CLASSIC SERMONS

Twelve Timeless Messages

ISBN 1-58660-740-5

Edited by Toni Sortor.

Scripture quotations are taken from the King James
Version of the Bible.

Published by Barbour Publishing, Inc., P.O. Box 719,
Uhrichsville, Ohio 44683, www.barbourbooks.com

*Our mission is to publish and distribute inspirational products
offering exceptional value and biblical encouragement to the
masses.*

Member of the
Evangelical Christian
Publishers Association

Printed in the United States of America.
5 4 3 2 1

CLASSIC
SERMONS

Contents

INTRODUCTION

The world has changed dramatically in the last few centuries, but the enduring message of Christianity has not. That message has been aptly chronicled by many powerful preachers in many memorable sermons—sermons worthy of reading decades, or even centuries, after their first delivery.

This small book, *Classic Sermons,* contains abridged and lightly updated versions of twelve timeless sermons. The topics they cover are as vital today as the day they were written: sin, salvation, God's love, duty, temptation, the Second Coming, eternity, and more—from the likes of John Bunyan, Billy Sunday, Jonathan Edwards, and D. L. Moody.

Whether you're a student, a pastor, or simply a reader of great Christian literature, *Classic Sermons* is sure to provide you many timeless insights—and guidance for your Christian life.

MAN'S GODLESS STATE

SINNERS IN THE HANDS OF AN ANGRY GOD

Jonathan Edwards
(1703–1758)

Their foot shall slide in due time.
DEUTERONOMY 32:35

In this verse the vengeance of God is threatened on the unbelieving Israelites who were God's people and lived under the means of grace but remained void of counsel, having no understanding. The expression I have chosen for my text, "their foot shall slide in due time," seems to imply the following things relating to the punishment and destruction to which these wicked Israelites were exposed: It implies that they were always exposed to destruction, as one that stands or walks in slippery places is always exposed to fall. It implies that they were always exposed to sudden unexpected destruction. As he that walks in slippery places cannot foresee one moment whether he shall stand or fall the next; and when he does fall, he falls at once without warning. Another thing implied is that they are liable to fall of themselves, as he that stands or walks on slippery ground needs nothing but his own weight to throw him down.

It implies that the reason why they are not fallen already and do not fall now is that God's appointed time is not come. When that appointed time comes, their foot shall slide. Then they shall be left to fall; God will not hold them up in these slippery places any longer but will let them go, and they shall fall into destruction. There is nothing that keeps wicked men at any one moment out of hell but the mere pleasure of God. By the mere pleasure of God, I mean His sovereign pleasure, His arbitrary will, restrained by no obligation, hindered by no manner of difficulty.

God is able to cast wicked men into hell at any moment. The strongest have no power to resist Him. He is not only able to cast wicked men into hell, but He can easily do it. They are as great heaps of light chaff before the whirlwind or large quantities of dry stubble before devouring flames. We find it easy to tread on and crush a worm that we see crawling on the earth; thus easy is it for God, when He pleases, to cast His enemies down to hell. What are we, that we should think to stand before Him, at whose rebuke the earth trembles and before whom the rocks are thrown down? Divine justice never stands in the way, it makes no objection against God's using His power at any moment to destroy them. On the contrary, justice calls for an infinite punishment of their sins. The sword of divine justice is every moment brandished over their heads, and it is nothing but the hand of arbitrary mercy and God's mere will that holds it back.

They are already under a sentence of condemnation to hell. They not only justly deserve to be cast down thither, but the sentence of the law of God is gone out against them and stands against them. John 3:18: "He that believeth not is condemned already." Every unconverted man belongs to hell; that is his place; from thence he is.

They are now the objects of that very same anger and wrath that is expressed in the torments of hell. And the reason why they do not go down to hell at each moment is not because God is not angry with them. It is not because God is unmindful of their wickedness and does not resent it that He does not let loose His hand and cut them off. The wrath of God burns against them, the pit is prepared, the fire is made ready, the furnace is now hot, ready to receive them; the flames do now rage and glow. The glittering sword is whet and held over them, and the pit hath opened its mouth under them.

The devil stands ready to fall upon them and seize them as his own as soon as God permits him. They belong to him; he has their souls in his possession and under his dominion. The Scripture represents them as his goods. The devils watch them; they are ever by them at their right hand; they stand waiting for them, like greedy, hungry lions that see their prey and expect to have it, but are for the present kept back. If God should withdraw His hand by which they are restrained, they would in one moment fly upon their poor souls. For the present, God restrains their wickedness by His mighty power, as He does the raging waves of the troubled sea, saying, "Hitherto shalt thou come, but no further"; but if God should withdraw that restraining power, it would soon carry all before it.

The bow of God's wrath is bent, the arrow made

ready on the string, and justice bends the arrow at your heart and strains the bow. It is nothing but the mere pleasure of God—and that of an angry God, without any promise or obligation at all—that keeps the arrow from being made drunk with your blood. All you that never passed under a great change of heart by the mighty power of the Spirit of God upon your souls; all you that were never born again and made new creatures and raised from being dead in sin to a state of new, and altogether inexperienced light and life, are in the hands of an angry God.

The God that holds you over the pit abhors you and is dreadfully provoked: His wrath toward you burns like fire; He looks upon you as worthy of nothing else but to be cast into the fire. You have offended Him, yet nothing but His hand holds you from falling into the fire every moment. It is to be ascribed to nothing else that you did not go to hell the last night; that you were allowed to awake again in this world after you closed your eyes to sleep. There is nothing else that is to be given as a reason why you do not this very moment drop down into hell. O sinner! Consider the fearful danger you are in: It is a great furnace of wrath, a wide and bottomless pit that you are held over in the hand of God, whose wrath is provoked and incensed as much against you as against many of the damned in hell. You hang by a slender thread, and nothing that you ever have done, nothing that you can do, will induce God to spare you one moment.

Consider this, you that are here yet remain in an

unregenerate state. That God will execute the fierceness of His anger implies that He will inflict wrath without any pity. He will have no regard to your welfare; nothing shall be withheld because it is too hard for you to bear. How awful are the words of Isaiah 63:3, "I will tread them in mine anger, and trample them in my fury; and their blood shall be sprinkled upon my garments, and I will stain all my raiment." God hath had it on His heart to show angels and men both how excellent His love is and also how terrible His wrath is. Thus it will be with you that are in an unconverted state. If you continue in it; the infinite might and majesty and terribleness of the omnipotent God shall be magnified upon you, in the ineffable strength of your torments. You shall be tormented in the presence of the holy angels and in the presence of the Lamb; and when you shall be in this state of suffering, the glorious inhabitants of heaven shall go forth and look on the awful spectacle, that they may see what the wrath and fierceness of the Almighty is; and when they have seen it, they will fall down and adore that great power and majesty.

How dreadful is the state of those in danger of this great wrath and infinite misery! But this is the dismal case of every soul in this congregation that has not been born again. Oh, that you would consider it, whether you be young or old! Many in this congregation will actually be the subjects of this very misery. It would be a wonder if some that are now present should not be in hell in a very short time, even before this year is out. The lost are past all hope; but here you are in the land

LOVE OF THE WORLD

Charles G. Finney
(1792–1875)

*Love not the world, neither the things that
are in the world. If any man love the world,
the love of the Father is not in him.*
1 JOHN 2:15

What are we to understand by the love of the world?

The love of the world spoken of here is not every
kind or degree of desire for worldly objects. God has so
constituted us that a certain amount and certain kinds
of worldly objects are indispensable to our existence.
We need food and raiment, implements of husbandry
and trade, and various worldly things. The proper
desire of these things is not sinful nor inconsistent with
the love of God. To love the world is to make worldly
things the principal objects of desire and pursuit. To
desire them more than to glorify God and save the
souls of men is to love the world. Where the love of
God and of men is supreme in the heart, there may be
a suitable desire for worldly objects, but where an indi-
vidual manifests a disposition to give the acquisition of
wealth or of worldly objects the preference, and aims
rather at obtaining worldly things than at glorifying
God and doing good to men, it is certain that the love
of the world is supreme in his heart.

Who does this? All who cheat and defraud to obtain the things of the world. That a man who will cheat and defraud his neighbor does not love his neighbor as himself is too manifest to require proof. That a man who will disobey God for the purpose of obtaining worldly goods does not love God supremely is self-evident. That he loves the things of the world supremely is a simple matter of fact. All those whose anxieties and cares are mostly about worldly things love the world supremely.

You that practice fraud and take advantage of the ignorance of men and cheat them in little or great things, do you pretend to love God? If so, you are an arrant hypocrite. And you who are filled with cares about worldly things—whose time and thoughts and affections are swallowed up in efforts to obtain them—know assuredly that you love the world and that the love of God is not in you.

All those who consult only their own interest in the transaction of business love the world supremely. God says, "Let every one look not upon his own things, but upon the things of others." "Let every one seek not his own, but another's wealth." These are express requirements of God; they are the very spirit and substance of the gospel. Suppose a man aims only at promoting his own interest and seeks not another's, but his own wealth. His only object is to take care of himself. This is the very opposite of the spirit of the gospel. Now let me ask you, can you deny this principle? What then is your spiritual state? Have you the love of God in you? How do you transact business? Be honest, try yourself by this rule; see whether you love your neighbor as yourself; see whether you love God supremely. Have you the spirit and temper of that God who lays down this rule of action? If not, you have not the love of God in you.

All who sell hurtful articles for the sake of the profit have not the love of God in them. The man that will sell articles of known pernicious tendency to his fellowmen for the sake of gain has the very spirit of hell. Shall a man who will sell rum or make whiskey pretend to love God?

All those who transact business upon principles of commercial justice rather than on principles of benevolence love the world supremely. Business principles are the principles of supreme selfishness. Upon these principles it is demanded that everyone take care of himself. Can a man love God supremely—and his neighbor as himself—who daily and habitually transacts business upon the principles of commercial justice?

All those who engage in business to the neglect of spiritual exercises love the world supremely. Many professors of religion seem just about as much determined to do good with their money as impenitent sinners are to repent. The only way in which money can be used for the glory of God and the good of men is to promote the spirituality and holiness of men. If you pursue business in a way that is inconsistent with your own spirituality, you might as well talk of getting drunk or swearing for the glory of God, as of making money for His glory. To be so busy in making money as to neglect to make personal efforts for the conversion of sinners is absurd.

All rich men love the world supremely. If they did not, they would not be rich. If they loved the kingdom of God supremely, they would give their riches to promote that kingdom. We always do what we generally choose to do. If a man loves the Lord Jesus Christ and the souls of men more than he does his money; if, upon the whole, he prefers the glory of God and the salvation of men to his own selfish interest, it is certain that he will cease to be rich and give his money to promote those objects. To say that he is rich but does not set his heart upon riches—that he continues to retain his wealth and yet does not set his heart upon it—is manifestly absurd and false.

All those who lay up their surplus income have not the love of God in them. By surplus income, I mean that which is not necessary for the support of themselves and families. If they lay it up, it must be because they love it. If they preferred the kingdom of Jesus Christ, they would immediately use what they could spare, after providing for the necessities of their families, to the building up of His kingdom.

All those who are more interested in secular news than in the accounts of revivals of religion, and in those things that pertain more particularly to the kingdom of Christ, love the world supremely. All those who would sooner engage in monied speculations than they would in revivals of religion love the world supremely. The naked matter of fact is, that if they prefer monied speculations to revivals of religion, they love money and love the world supremely.

All those who do not feel more gratified with the appropriation of money to the cause of Christ than with any other appropriation of it love the world supremely. A man who loves God and longs for the coming of His kingdom will feel gratified with appropriating money for the promotion of that darling object.

All those who would rather see a customer come in to pay them money than an agent of some benevolent society to receive and appropriate it to the promotion of Christ's kingdom love the world supremely. This demonstrates, beyond all doubt, where his heart is and shows that he loves his money more than he loves his God.

All those who do not really enjoy giving more than receiving love the world supremely. If they loved God supremely, their supreme object and joy in receiving would be that they might immediately turn round and give to the promotion of their darling object.

All those who are more parsimonious in their expenditures for the kingdom of Christ than in their expenditures upon themselves and their families love the world supremely. Men are always most free in appropriating their money to the promotion of the objects dearest to their hearts. This is a simple matter of fact. If, therefore, the heart is set supremely upon honoring God with our substance, it is certain that if in anything we are bountiful and liberal in our expenditures, it will be in fitting up places for His worship and in all those things that are essential to decency, to comfort, and enjoyment in His service.

It is impossible that a man should have two supreme objects of affection. If he have any acceptable love to God, it must be supreme. To affirm that a man loves the world and God with any acceptable love is a contradiction. It is the same as to say that he loves both God and the world supremely. A man cannot love two objects that are entirely opposite to each other at the same time. The love of the world and the love of God are directly opposite states of mind, so that to exercise them both at the same time is impossible.

Perhaps some of you will say, if the doctrine of this sermon be true, who can be saved? I answer, certainly not those who manage their affairs upon principles that are in direct opposition to the benevolence of the gospel; who satisfy themselves with being honest in this sense of honesty, instead of being governed by the law of love; who seek their own and not their neighbor's wealth; who mind earthly things and account it more blessed to receive than to give. If there be any truth in the Word of God, all such men are in the way to hell. But will anyone object and say, this is very uncharitable. If this be true, nearly all the church are hypocrites. I answer, the doctrine is true, whatever the inference may be.

SALVATION

IMMEASURABLE LOVE

Charles H. Spurgeon
(1834–1892)

For God so loved the world, that he gave
his only begotten Son, that whosoever
believeth in him should not perish,
but have everlasting life.
JOHN 3:16

Come, ye aged saints, be children again; and you that
have long known your Lord, take up your first spelling
book and go over your ABCs again, by learning that
God so loved the world, that He gave His Son to die,
that man might live through Him. I do not call you to
an elementary lesson because you have forgotten your
letters, but because it is a good thing to refresh the
memory and a blessed thing to feel young again.

"God so loved the world." What was there in the
world that God should love it? There was nothing lov-
able in it. No fragrant flower grew in that arid desert.
Enmity to Him, hatred to His truth, disregard of His
law, rebellion against His commandments—those were
the thorns and briars which covered the wasteland; but
no desirable thing blossomed there. Yet, "God loved the
world," says the text. So divinely did He love it that He
gave His only Son to redeem the world from perishing
and to gather out of it a people to His praise. Whence

came that love? He loves because it is His nature to do so. The world had sadly gone astray because of its offenses; and there was need for help.

I might handle my text in a thousand different ways, but for simplicity's sake, and to keep to the one point of setting forth the love of God, I want to make you see how great that love is by five different particulars.

The first is the GIFT: Consider what this gift was that God gave. It was His only begotten Son—His beloved Son, in whom He was well pleased. When God gave God for us, He gave Himself. What more could He give? If you desire to see the love of God in this great procedure you must consider how He gave His Son. The Lord God sent the Heir of all things to toil in a carpenter's shop: to drive the nail and push the plane and use the saw. He sent Him down amongst scribes and Pharisees, whose cunning eyes watched Him and whose cruel tongues scourged Him. He sent Him down to hunger and thirst, amid poverty so dire that He had not where to lay His head. He sent Him down to the scourging and the crowning with thorns. At length He gave Him up to death—a felon's death, the death of the crucified. He gave Him to be made a curse for us; gave Him that He might die "the just for the unjust, to bring us to God."

"God so loved the world, that he gave his only begotten Son." When did He do that? From before the foundation of the world. The promise of Jesus was made in the garden of Eden almost as soon as Adam fell. Throughout the ages the great Father stood to His gift. He looked upon His Only Begotten as man's hope. Every sacrifice was God's renewal of His gift of grace, a reassurance that He had bestowed the gift and would never draw back therefrom.

As this gift refers not only to our Lord's death but to the ages before it, so it includes also all the ages afterwards. God "so loved the world that he gave"—and still gives—"his only begotten Son, that whosoever believeth in him should not perish, but have everlasting life." The Lord is giving Christ away tonight. Will anyone refuse? This good gift, this perfect gift—can you decline it? If you can but hold out your empty willing hand, the Lord will give Christ to you at this moment.

> Dear dying Lamb, Thy precious blood
> Shall never lose its power
> 'Til all the ransomed church of God
> Be saved to sin no more.

Now notice the love of God in THE PLAN OF SALVATION. He has put it thus: "that whosoever believeth on him should not perish, but have everlasting life." The way of salvation is extremely simple to understand and exceedingly easy to practice. Trust in Christ is the certain way of eternal happiness. What is it to believe in Jesus? It is this: to trust yourself with Him. If your hearts are ready, though you have never believed in Jesus before, I trust you will believe in Him now. O Holy Spirit, graciously make it so.

What is it to believe in Jesus? It is, first, to give your

firm and cordial assent to the truth that God did send His Son, born of a woman, to stand in the room and stead of guilty men, and that God did cause to meet on Him the iniquities of us all, so that He bore the punishment due to our transgressions, being made a curse for us. Oh, that you may rejoice that this is true and be thankful that such a blessed fact is revealed by God Himself. Jesus has offered an atonement, and that atonement becomes yours when you accept it by putting your trust in Him. I want you now to say,

> My faith doth lay her hand
> On that dear head of Thine
> While, like a penitent, I stand,
> And here confess my sin.

Thirdly, the love of God shines forth with transcendent brightness. THE PERSONS FOR WHOM THIS PLAN IS AVAILABLE and for whom this gift is given are "Whosoever believeth in him." While every unbeliever is excluded, every believer is included. Suppose a man has been guilty of all the lusts of the flesh. If that man shall believe in Jesus Christ, he shall at once be made clean from his defilement and shall not perish because of his sin. But, says one, "I take exception to the salvation of this wicked wretch. He has behaved so abominably that in all justice he ought to be sent to hell." Just so. But if he repents of his sin and believes in the Lord Jesus Christ, he shall not be sent there. He shall be changed in character, so that he shall never perish but have eternal life.

This "whosoever" makes a grand sweep, for it encircles all degrees of faith. It may be that he has no full assurance; it may be that he has no assurance at all; but if he has faith, true and childlike, by it he shall be saved. Though his faith be so little that I must needs put on my spectacles to see it, yet Christ will see it and reward it.

My faith is feeble, I confess,
I faintly trust Thy word;
But wilt Thou pity me the less?
Be that far from Thee, Lord!

Now fourthly, another beam of divine love is to be seen in the negative blessing here stated, namely, in THE DELIVERANCE implied in the words, "that whosoever believeth in him should not perish."

Whosoever with his heart believeth in Christ is a saved man, not for tonight only, but for all the nights that ever shall be, shall have a life that cannot die, a justification that cannot be disputed, an acceptance which shall never cease.

What is it to perish? It is to lose all hope in Christ, all trust in God, all light in life, all peace in death, all joy, all bliss, all union with God. This shall never happen if thou believest in Christ. He that hath union with Christ has union with perfection, omnipotence, and glory. He that believeth in Jesus is united to Him, and he must live because Jesus lives. The man who is in Christ will not live in sin or return to his old sins for the grace of God will continue to save him from his sins. As only God can create, so only God can destroy; and He will never destroy the work of His own hands.

The last commendation of His love lies in the positive—IN THE POSSESSION. God gives every man that believes in Christ everlasting life. When I first received everlasting life I had no idea what a treasure had come to me. I knew that I had obtained something very extraordinary, but of its superlative value I was not aware.

You are not a saved man unless Christ has saved you forever. That which has such a grip on you is the power of God. To have Christ living in you and the truth ingrained in your very nature, this is the thing that saves the soul, and nothing short of it. It is written in the text "God so loved the world, that he gave his only begotten Son, that whosoever believeth in him should not perish, but have everlasting life." As long as there is a God, the believer shall not only exist, but live. As long as there is a heaven, you shall enjoy it; as long as there is a Christ, you shall live in His love; and as long as there is an eternity, you shall continue to fill it with delight.

God bless you and help you to believe in Jesus. Amen.

LAST SERMON

John Bunyan
(1628–1688)

Which were born, not of blood,
nor of the will of the flesh,
nor of the will of man,
but of God.
JOHN 1:13

The words have a dependence on what goes before, and therefore I must direct you to them for the right understanding of it. You have it thus: "He came unto his own, and his own received him not; but as many as received him, to them gave he power to become the sons of God, even to them which believe on his name; which were born, not of blood, nor of the will of the flesh, but of God." In these words, you have two things: First, some of His own rejecting Him when He offered Himself to them, and secondly, others of His own receiving Him and making Him welcome. Those that reject Him, He passes by; but those that receive Him, He gives the power to become the sons of God. They that did not receive Him were only born of flesh and blood; but those that receive Him have God as their father, they receive the doctrine of Christ with a vehement desire.

First, I will show you what [John] means by "blood." They that believe are born to it, as an heir is

31

to an inheritance; they are born of God; not of flesh, nor of the will of man, but of God; not of blood—that is, not by generation; not born to the kingdom of heaven by the flesh; not because I am the son of a godly man or woman. That is meant by blood, Acts 17:26, He has "made of one blood all nations." But when he says here, "not of blood," he rejects all carnal privileges they did boast of. They boasted they were Abraham's seed. No, no, says he, it is not of blood; think not to say you have Abraham to your father, you must be born of God if you go to the kingdom of heaven.

Secondly, "Nor of the will of the flesh." What must we understand by that?

Men are not made the children of God by fulfilling their lustful desires; it must be understood here in the best sense. There is not only in carnal men a will to be vile, but there is in them a will to be saved also—a will to go to heaven. But this will not privilege a man in the things of the kingdom of God. Natural desires are not an argument to prove a man shall go to heaven whenever he dies. I am not a free-willer, I do abhor it; yet there is not the wickedest man but desires at some time or other to be saved. A man without grace, though he have natural gifts, yet he shall not obtain privilege to go to heaven and be the son of God. Though a man without grace may have a will to be saved, yet he cannot have that will God's way. Nature cannot know anything but the things of nature; the things of God know no man but by the Spirit of God. Unless the Spirit of God be in you, it will leave you on this side the gates of heaven.

Men that believe in Jesus Christ to the effectual receiving of Jesus Christ are born to it. "Except a man be born again, he cannot see the kingdom of God." Unless he be born of God, he cannot see it. Believing is the consequence of the new birth, "not of blood, nor of the will of man, but of God."

A child, before it be born into the world, is in the dark dungeon of its mother's womb. So a child of God, before he be born again, is in the dark dungeon of sin. He sees nothing of the kingdom of God, therefore it is called a new birth.

I must give you a few consequences of a new birth. First of all, a child cries as soon as it comes into the world. If there is no noise, they say it is dead. You that are born of God, and Christians, if you be not criers, there is no spiritual life in you. As soon as He has raised you out of the dark dungeon of sin, you cannot but cry to God, "What must I do to be saved?" Secondly, it is not only natural for a child to cry, but it must also crave the breast. It cannot live without the breast; therefore Peter makes it the true trial of a newborn babe; the newborn babe desires the sincere milk of the Word, that he may grow thereby. If you be born of God, make it manifest by desiring the breast of God. If you be born again, there is no satisfaction 'til you get the milk of God's Word into your souls; Isaiah 66:11, "To suck, and be satisfied with the breasts of consolation. . ."

Thirdly, a child that is newly born, if it have not

other comforts to keep it warm, it dies. So those that are born again must have some promise to keep them alive. And when women are with child, what fine things will they prepare for their child! O but what fine things has Christ prepared to wrap all in that are born again!

Fourthly, when a child is in its mother's lap, the mother takes great delight to have that which will be for its comfort. So it is with God's children; they shall be kept on His knee; Isaiah 66:11, "That ye may suck, and be satisfied with the breasts of her consolations." Verse 13, "As one whom his mother comforteth, so will I comfort you." There is a similitude in these things that nobody knows of but those that are born again.

Fifthly, there is usually some similitude between the father and the child. It may be the child looks like its father. So those that are born again have the image of Jesus Christ (Galatians 4). Everyone that is born of God has something of the features of heaven upon him. Men usually love those children that are like them. So does God His children; therefore they are called the children of God. But others do not look like Him, therefore they are called Sodomites. If you are earthly, you have borne the image of the earthly; if heavenly, you have borne the image of the heavenly.

Sixthly, when a man has a child, he trains him up to his own liking. The child learns the custom of his father's house. Those that are born of God have learned the custom of the true church of God, there they learn to cry, My Father and my God; they are brought up in

God's house, they learn the method and form of God's house for regulating their lives in this world.

Seventhly, it is natural for children to depend upon their father for what they want. If they want a pair of shoes, they go and tell him; if they want bread, they go and tell him. So should the children of God do. Do you want spiritual bread? Go tell God of it. Do you want strength of grace? Ask it of God. Do you want strength against Satan's temptations? Go and tell God of it. When the devil tempts you, run home and tell your heavenly Father; go pour out your complaints to God. This is natural to children; if any wrong them, they go and tell their father; so do those that are born of God, when they meet with temptations, go and tell God of them.

If you be risen with Christ, set your affections on things above, and not on things below. When you come together, talk of what your Father promised you; you should all love your Father's will, and be content and pleased with the exercises you meet with in the world. If you are the children of God, live together lovingly. If the world quarrel with you, it is no matter; but it is sad if you quarrel together. If this be amongst you, it is a sign of ill-breeding, it is not according to rules you have in the Word of God. Dost thou see a soul that has the image of God in him? Love him, love him; say, This man and I must go to heaven one day. Serve one another, do good for one another; and if any wrong you, pray to God to right you, and love the brotherhood.

Lastly, if you are the children of God, learn this

lesson: "Gird up the loins of your mind as obedient children, not fashioning yourselves according to your former conversation; but be ye holy in all manner of conversation." Consider that the holy God is your Father, and let this oblige you to live like the children of God, that you may look your Father in the face with comfort another day.

Marks of a True Conversion

George Whitefield
(1714–1770)

Verily I say unto you,
Except ye be converted,
and become as little children,
ye shall not enter into the kingdom of heaven.
Matthew 18:3

I suppose I may take it for granted that all of you are fully convinced that it is appointed for all men once to die and that ye all really believe that after death comes the judgment, and that the consequences of that judgment will be that ye must be doomed to dwell in the blackness of darkness or ascend to dwell with the blessed God forever and ever. There are many who go on in a round of duties, a model of performances, thinking they shall go to heaven. But if you examine them, though they have a Christ in their heads, they have no Christ in their hearts. The Lord Jesus Christ knew this full well; He knew how desperately wicked and deceitful men's hearts are. The Lord plainly tells us what great change must be wrought in us, and what must be done for us, before we can have any well-grounded hopes of entering into the kingdom of heaven. He tells Nicodemus that "unless a man be born again, and from above, and unless a man be born of water and of the Spirit, he cannot enter into the kingdom of God." The words, if you look back to the context, are plainly directed to the disciples, for we are told "that at the same time came the disciples unto Jesus." I think it is plain from many parts of Scripture that these disciples were in some degree converted before. If we take the words strictly, they are applicable only to those that have already gotten some faith in Christ—though but weak. Though they had already tasted the grace of God, yet there was so much of the old man, so much indwelling sin and corruption remaining in their hearts, that unless they were more converted than they were, they could give very little evidence of belonging to His kingdom.

Before you or I can have any well-grounded, scriptural hope of being happy in a future state, there must be some great, notable, and amazing change upon our souls. Not one adult person in the congregation would deny that a great change hath passed upon their bodies since they came into the world. Though you are in one respect the same, a person that knew you when you were in your cradle would hardly know you at all today. Before we can go to heaven, there must be a great change upon our souls. Our souls are still the same in a physical sense, but our temper, habit, and conduct must be so changed that those who knew us before and are acquainted with us now must stand amazed.

Too many who have been baptized in the name of Christ dare to speak against the doctrine of original sin and are angry with those ill-natured ministers who paint man in such black colors. Say they, "It cannot be that children come into the world with the guilt of Adam's sin lying upon them." That little children are guilty, that they are conceived and born in sin, is plain from the whole tenor of the book of God. It is plain from Scripture and the fact that children are born in sin and consequently are children of wrath. I think that the death of every child is a plain proof of original sin. Sickness and death came into the world by sin, and it seems not consistent with God's goodness and justice to let a little child be sick or die unless Adam's first sin was imputed to him. If any charge God with injustice for imputing Adam's sin to a little child, behold we have gotten a second Adam to bring our children to Him. Little children are innocent, compared with grown people, but take them as they are, and they have hearts that are sensual and minds which are carnal. I mention this with the greatest concern because I believe that unless parents are convinced of this, they will never take proper care of their children's education.

Do not mistake me, I am not going to persuade you to shut up your shops or leave your business; I am not going to persuade you to retire from the world. No, the religion of Jesus is a social religion. But though Jesus Christ does not call us to go out of the world, shut up our shops, and leave our children to be provided for by miracles, yet this must be said to the honor of Christianity: If we are really converted, we shall be loose from the world. Though we are engaged in it and obliged to work for our children; though we are obliged to follow trades and merchandise and to be serviceable to the commonwealth, if we are real Christians, we shall be loose to the world; though I will not pretend to say that all real Christians have attained to the same degree of spiritual-mindedness.

When our Lord says we must be converted and become as little children, I suppose He also means that we must be sensible of our weakness, comparatively speaking, as a little child led by the hand. Those that are converted look upon themselves as ignorant. Christ's flock is called a little flock not only because it's little in number, but also because members of His flock are little in their own eyes. Hence the apostle Paul, when he speaks of himself, says, "Unto me, who am less than the least of all saints, is this grace given, that I should preach among the Gentiles the unsearchable riches of Christ."

If we are converted and become as little children, we shall be guileless as well as harmless. Do not mistake me; I am not saying that Christians ought not to be prudent, otherwise they may follow the delusions of the devil. A great man lamented, "God has given me many gifts, but God has not given me prudence." When I say a Christian must be guileless, I do not mean he should lie open to everyone's assault: We should pray for the wisdom of the serpent, though we shall generally learn this wisdom by our blunders and imprudence.

Hark, O man! Hark, O woman! He that hath ears to hear, let him hear what the Lord Jesus Christ says. "Verily I say unto you, except ye be converted, and become as little children, ye shall not enter into the kingdom of heaven." This is Saturday night, and you are now preparing for the Sabbath, but you may yet never live to see the Sabbath. You have had awful proofs of this lately; a woman died but yesterday, a man died the day before, another was killed by something that fell from a house, and it may be in twenty-four hours more, many of you may be carried into an unalterable state. Now then, for God's sake, for your own soul's sake, if you have a mind to dwell with God and cannot bear the thought of dwelling in everlasting burning, before I go any further, silently put up one prayer, or say Amen to the prayer I would put in your mouths: "Lord, search me and try me; Lord, examine my heart, and let my conscience speak; O let me know whether I am converted or not!"

If you art thus converted and become a little child, I welcome you, in the name of the Lord Jesus, into God's dear family. I welcome you, in the name of the dear Redeemer, into the company of God's children. Then what must you do? My dear hearers, be obedient to God. If God be your Father, obey Him: If God be your Father, serve Him; love Him with all your heart, love Him with all your might, with all your soul, and with all your strength. Deal with God as your little children do with you. Does the devil trouble you? Does the world trouble you? Go tell your Father of it, go directly and complain to God. The Lord will then speak for you some way or other.

Are you converted and become as little children? Have you entered into God's family? Then assure yourselves that your heavenly Father will chasten you now and then: "For what son is there whom the father chasteneth not: if ye are without chastisement, of which all are partakers, then are ye bastards and not sons." If you are converted and become as little children, do not expect that God will be a foolish parent. No, how did He correct Miriam? how did He correct Moses? How hath God in all ages corrected His dearest children?

Though I have been speaking comfortably, what I have been saying belongs to children. If any of you are graceless, Christless, unconverted creatures, I charge you not to touch the bread of life 'til you are turned to Jesus Christ. I suppose many of you are unconverted and graceless. Go home! Get away to your closets and down with your stubborn hearts before God. If you have not done it before, let this be the night. Or begin now, while standing here. Pray to God, and let the language of your heart be: Lord, convert me! Lord, make me a little child, Lord Jesus, let me not be banished from Thy kingdom! My dear friends, there is a great deal more implied in the words than is expressed: when Christ says, "Ye shall not enter into the kingdom of heaven." It is as much to say, "you shall certainly go to hell, you shall certainly be damned, and dwell in the blackness of darkness forever."

CHRISTIAN DUTY

Stewardship

Charles G. Finney
(1792–1875)

Give an account of thy stewardship.
Luke 16:2

A steward is employed to transact the business of another as his agent or representative. His duty is to promote the interest of his employer. He may be called to account for the manner in which he has transacted his business and to be removed from his office at the pleasure of his employer.

One important design of the parable is to teach that all men are God's stewards. The Bible declares that the silver and the gold are His and that He is, in the highest possible sense, the Proprietor of the universe. Men are mere stewards, employed by Him for the transaction of His business, and required to do all they do for His glory.

That men are God's stewards is evident because God treats them as such, removes them at His pleasure, and disposes of the property in their hands, which He could not do did He not consider them His agents, not the owners of the property.

If men are God's stewards, they are bound to account to Him for their time. God has created them and keeps them alive, and their time is His. Reader, would you not expect your steward to employ his time in your service? Suppose he were often idle? That would be bad enough, but suppose that when called to account and censured for not doing his duty, he should say, "Why, what have I done?" Would you not feel that letting your business suffer was great wickedness for which he deserved to be punished? Now, reader, you are God's steward, and if you are an impenitent sinner, you have wholly neglected God's business and have remained idle in His vineyard or have been attending to your own private interests.

Suppose your steward spent his time opposing your interest, using your capital and time in speculations directly opposed to the business for which he was employed? Would you not suppose yourself obliged to call him to account? And would you not account anyone a villain who should approve such conduct? Would you not think yourself bound to publish him abroad, that the world might know his character and you might clear yourself from the charge of upholding such a person?

How shall God dispose of you if you employ your time in opposing His interest and use His capital for speculations directly opposed to the business for which He has employed you? Will not God consider Himself under an obligation to call you to an account? Must He not feel Himself constrained to make you a public example, that the universe may know how much He abhors your crimes!

Stewards are bound to give an account of their

talents, the powers of their minds. Suppose you should educate a man to be your steward, should support him during the time he was engaged in study, and pay for the expense of his education—and then he should either neglect to employ his mind in your service or should use the powers of his cultivated intellect for the promotion of his own interests. Would you not consider this fraud? And do you, sinner, employ the powers of your mind and whatever education God may have given you in opposing His interest—perverting His truth—scattering "firebrands, arrows, and death" all around you, and think to escape His curse? Shall not the Almighty be avenged upon such a wretch?

A steward is bound to give an account for the influence he exerts upon mankind around him. Suppose you should employ a steward and he refused or neglected to promote your interest. Would you not consider this default a perpetual fraud practiced upon you? Reader, whatever influence God has given you, if you are an impenitent sinner, you are not only neglecting to use it for God to build up His kingdom, but you are employing it in opposition to His interest and glory; and for this do you not deserve the damnation of hell? Perhaps you are rich or learned or have, on other accounts, great influence in society and are refusing to use it to save the souls of men, but are bringing all your weight of character and talents and influence to drag all within the sphere of your influence down to the gates of hell.

Suppose your steward should refuse to employ the capital with which you intrusted him for the promotion of your interest or were to account it his own and use it for his own private interests, the gratification of his lusts, or the aggrandizement of his family, while at the same time your business was suffering for the want of this very capital. Or suppose that this steward held the purse strings of your wealth and you had other servants whose needs were to be supplied out of the means in his hands. Their welfare, even their lives, depended on these supplies; and yet this steward should minister to his own lusts and those of his family and allow your other servants to perish. What would you think of such wickedness?

But suppose your servant should say, "Have I not acquired this property by my own industry?" Would you not answer, "You have employed my capital to do it and my time, for which I have paid you; and the money you have gained is mine." So when God calls upon you to use the property in your possession for Him, do you say it is yours, that you have obtained it by your own industry? Whose time have you used, and whose talents and means?

God commands you to be a coworker with Him in converting the world. He needs your services, for He saves souls only through the agency of men. If souls are lost or the gospel is not spread over the world, sinners charge all the blame upon Christians, as if they only were bound to be active in the cause of Christ, to exercise benevolence, to pray for a lost world, to pull sinners out of the fire. Who has absolved you from these duties?

You must give an account of your opportunities of doing good. Now, sinner, you have always neglected opportunities of serving God, of warning your fellow sinners, of promoting revivals of religion, and advancing the interest of truth. You have been diligent merely to promote your own private interests and have entirely neglected the interests of your Employer. Do you not deserve to lose the stewardship as a dishonest man and be sent to prison? How can you escape the damnation of hell?

You can see why idleness is a snare to the soul. A man that is idle is dishonest; he forgets his responsibility, refuses to serve God, and gives himself up to the temptations of the devil. Nay, the idle man tempts the devil to tempt him. A maxim says that men cannot attend to business and religion at the same time. A man's business ought to be a part of his religion. He cannot be religious in idleness. He must have some business to be religious at all, and if it is performed from a right motive, his lawful and necessary business is as much a necessary part of religion as prayer or going to church or reading his Bible.

It is ridiculous to call institutions for the extension of the Redeemer's kingdom in the world "charitable institutions," although in one sense, they may be called such. Should you give your steward orders to appropriate a certain amount of funds for the benefit of the poor in a certain parish, this would be charity in you, but not in him. It would be ridiculous for him to pretend that the charity was his. Institutions for the promotion of religion are the charities of God, not of man. The funds are God's, and it is His requirement that they be expended, according to His directions, to relieve the misery or advance the happiness of our fellowmen. God is the giver.

We have a true test of Christian character. True Christians consider themselves God's stewards. They act for Him, live for Him, transact business for Him, eat and drink for His glory, live and die to please Him. But sinners and hypocrites live for themselves. They account their time, their talents, their influence, as their own and dispose of them all for their own private interest, thus drowning themselves in destruction and perdition.

At the judgment, we are informed that Christ will say to those who are accepted, "Well done, good and faithful servants." Reader! could He truly say this of you, "Well done, good and faithful servant; thou hast been faithful over a few things," i.e., over the things committed to your charge? He will pronounce no false judgment, put no false estimate upon things; and if He cannot say this truly, you will not be accepted but will be thrust down to hell. God will soon call you to give an account of your stewardship. Have you been faithful to God, faithful to your own soul and the souls of others? Are you ready to have your accounts examined, your conduct scrutinized, and your life weighed in the balance of the sanctuary? If not, repent, repent now of all your wickedness and lay hold upon the hope that is set before you; for, hark! a voice cries in your ears, "Give an account of thy stewardship for thou mayest be no longer steward."

On the Sabbath, Part 1

John Calvin
(1509–1564)

Keep the sabbath day to sanctify it,
as the LORD thy God hath commanded thee.
Six days thou shalt labour, and do all thy work:
But the seventh day is the sabbath of the LORD thy God:
in it thou shalt not do any work, thou, nor thy son, nor
thy daughter, nor thy manservant, nor thy maidservant,
nor thine ox, nor thine ass, nor any of thy cattle,
nor thy stranger that is within thy gates; that thy
manservant and thy maidservant may rest as well as thou.
DEUTERONOMY 5:12–14

The Sabbath was first a figure to show that men cannot serve God properly unless they put to death their own nature and dedicate themselves fully to Him so as to be separate from the world. Second, the day of rest was a ceremony to bring the people together to hear the Law, call upon the name of God, offer sacrifices, and do all other things that concern the spiritual government.

The Sabbath was a shadow under the Law until the coming of our Lord Jesus Christ, to make men understand that God requires them to cease from their own works. Colossians 2:17 says that we have in Jesus Christ the substance and the principal part of the things that were under the Law. Therefore it was necessary for the fathers of old to be trained in this hope by the day of rest and other ceremonies.

But now that the thing itself is given to us, we must not rest any longer in shadows. Indeed the Law is not abolished (Matthew 5:18; Ephesians 2:15; Colossians 1:14, 17), so we must hold now the substance and truth of it. Even so, the shadow of it is done away by the coming of our Lord Jesus Christ. If someone demands to know how the fathers of old knew that it was a shadow, the answer is that Moses gave them this understanding of it, as is shown sufficiently in Exodus 31:13 and 17. God, having given His Law to Moses (Exodus 20), tells him the purpose of the day, saying that He had ordained the Sabbath to be a warrant for the sanctifying of the people of Israel to Himself. When Scripture speaks of our being made holy to God, it means that we are to be separate from all things that are contrary to His service. In the world there is nothing but utter rebellion and sinfulness. When men follow their own thoughts, desires, wishes, and lusts, they make open war against God. We cannot serve Him without defilement unless we are separated from the defilement that is contrary to Him and the things of our nature are abolished.

All these things were shown as figures to the ancient fathers because Jesus Christ was not yet fully revealed to them, but now we have the full accomplishment and perfection of all things in Jesus Christ. Saint Paul says that the old man is crucified with Him (Romans 6:6). When Paul speaks of the old man he means the things that we have received from Adam, all of which must be done away. He is not speaking of the physical body or of the essence of the soul but of the sinfulness in us. The blindness that makes us go astray and the wicked lusts and passions which are utterly disobedient to God's righteousness must be beaten down because they have come from Adam. How is this to be done? By our Lord Jesus Christ, who has purchased this prerogative through the power of the Holy Spirit which enables us to forsake the world and ourselves. By this, our sinful desires shall not master us.

Although we are full of disobedience, yet God's Spirit rules over us to hold down the passions and keep them in subjection. But this was not yet made manifest under the Law. It was necessary that the fathers who lived at that time should have some help to nourish them in the hope of the death of our Lord Jesus Christ, that they might know their sins were washed away by the blood of the Mediator. Similarly, they had the Sabbath day as a warrant for the grace that was purchased for us so that God might live in us by the power of His Holy Spirit (Galatians 2:19–20). The Sabbath day was a figure to represent what was fulfilled in the coming of our Lord Jesus Christ. Therefore let us note that the Sabbath applied to the whole service to God to show men that they could not honor Him in a pure manner unless they renounced themselves and were separated from the defiling aspects of the world and their own sinful nature.

Therefore we must come to the important point

of this: To serve God properly, we must learn to give up our wills, thoughts, and desires. We must lay down our own "wisdom" and hear God speak without following our own will or fancy.

The first way to keep the Sabbath as we should is to give up the things that seem good to ourselves. We must continue quietly in obedience to God. The purpose is that we should live in holy obedience to God by receiving His simple word and fashioning our lives according to His righteousness. When we hear God commanding us to keep the Sabbath day, we must be firm with ourselves. We will profit throughout our lives if we keep the Sabbath well by renouncing whatever is our own and dedicating ourselves entirely to God.

The things that are ordained concerning the Sabbath day are now fulfilled, at least with respect to the truth of the figure that the fathers had only as a shadow. What was commanded about the day of rest must also apply to us, for we must take God's law as it is and thus have an everlasting rule of righteousness. The apostle (Hebrews 4:3–10) applies the things that were spoken about the Sabbath to the instruction of the Christians of the new Church. He shows us that we must imitate our God in whom reside happiness and perfection, because the entire sovereign welfare (or highest good) of man consists in being created in the image of God.

Do we think that God ever took pleasure in man's idleness? Surely not! Rather He punished as severely the person who worked on the Sabbath day as He did a murderer. It seems to be a cruel thing that a man should be put to death for chopping a little wood on the Sabbath day, as in Numbers 15:32–35, as if he had committed murder. And yet God does condemn to death the one who cut wood on the Sabbath day because under this figure is included the whole service to God. The same applies to those in Jeremiah (7:18–20, 28) who carried loads and drove their carts on the Sabbath day.

Since we aren't constrained by the figure and God has given us greater liberty, let us learn to give ourselves wholeheartedly to Him. God must govern us completely, and we must sincerely desire nothing other than rest in Him. For this reason, God sets forth Himself as an example. After He had created the world and everything in it, He rested. He didn't rest because He was weary or because He had a need to rest, but rather to direct our attention to His works so we might rest in them and, having considered them, model ourselves after Him.

Let us understand that God's ordaining the seventh day for rest was not without cause. He makes it clear that we cannot attain to perfect holiness in a day, let alone in a month. Even when we have fought heartily against the desires of our sinful nature and against our wicked thoughts, there will always remain some dregs that will remain until we have been united with our God and He has taken us up to His heavenly kingdom.

We must apply this rest to a higher purpose. We must refrain from our business, call upon His name, and exercise ourselves in His Word. When the stores are closed on the Lord's Day and men do not travel about as they do on other days, we have more leisure and liberty to attend to the things that God commands. We can be taught by His Word, meet together for the confession of our faith, call upon His name, and exercise ourselves in the proper use of the sacraments. This is how the Sabbath should serve us.

It is not enough for us to meditate upon God and His works on the Lord's Day by ourselves. We must meet together on a specified day to perform the public confession of our faith. This should be done every day, but because of man's spiritual immaturity and laziness it is necessary to have a special day dedicated entirely to this purpose. It is best that we keep the regulation that God has commanded, come together in the company of the faithful, and show the agreement we have with the whole body of the Church.

Let us consider the purpose of our Lord's command to the people of old that they should have one day of rest a week. Since we know that the day has been abolished by the coming of the Lord Jesus Christ, we should ensure that we apply ourselves to the spiritual rest. That is, we should dedicate ourselves entirely to God, forsaking all our own ideas and desires. But we should retain the outward regulation, as it is useful for putting aside our own affairs and business so that we can apply ourselves entirely to the meditation of God's works and occupy ourselves in a consideration of the good things that He has done for

On the Sabbath, Part 2

John Calvin
(1509–1564)

Six days thou shalt labour, and do all thy work:
But the seventh day is the sabbath of the LORD thy God:
in it thou shalt not do any work, thou, nor thy son, nor
thy daughter, nor thy manservant, nor thy maidservant,
nor thine ox, nor thine ass, nor any of thy cattle,
nor thy stranger that is within thy gates; that thy
manservant and thy maidservant may rest as well as thou.
And remember that thou wast a servant in the land of
Egypt, and that the LORD thy God brought thee out
thence through a mighty hand and by a stretched out arm:
therefore the LORD thy God commanded thee
to keep the sabbath day.
DEUTERONOMY 5:13–15

Since our Lord Jesus Christ has fulfilled the commandment perfectly for us, we must not dwell upon the shadow of the Law (Romans 6:6). Rather, we should be content with crucifying the old man through the power of the suffering and death of our Lord Jesus Christ so that we can be completely renewed in our service to God. Yet we need regulation and order among ourselves. It was necessary that a day of rest be appointed for us to meet together, that we may be confirmed in the doctrines of God and profit from them every day. The Day also serves for calling on His name and confessing our faith.

It is impossible for us to keep the Law of God. Even if a man wished to keep it, he wouldn't know where to begin. If it were possible for men to keep the Law under their own power, the command would be: Work, but instead, the command is: Rest, so God may work. The key point of the text is that God gives man some comfort. Seeing our lack of discipline and weaknesses and our inability to fulfill our duties, God releases us from the most severe rigor by saying that He is satisfied with our giving Him one day. If that day serves us for the entire week, He is satisfied with that. Let us guard ourselves so that nothing can keep us from following the path that God directs for us. Although by nature we strive against His ways, let us nevertheless resist striving and press on, being always fully obedient to our God.

Now we have an important message that speaks about male and female servants. God reminds the Jews that they were servants in Egypt and should be gentle with those who are under their authority. Thus, He says, "your male and female servants are to rest." Why? "Because you yourselves were once slaves, and at that time you wished that someone would have given you rest and relief. Because of this, you must be gentle with those under your hand." From this it appears that God ordained the Sabbath Day not only as a spiritual regulation but out of kindness, for He says: "You must be gentle with others."

There are two main sections in God's Law: One deals with our duties to Him, and the other concerns our duty towards our neighbors. The purpose of the two sections is that they should serve as the reference point for our entire life. With respect to the fact that we belong to God: We are to walk in obedience to Him, particularly since we receive our life from Him; pay homage to Him since He created us for a better hope, adopted us as His children, and has redeemed us with the blood of His Son; be entirely His, striving to withdraw ourselves from the pollution of this world so that we can be true sacrifices to Him and call on Him alone, fleeing only to Him for comfort; and give Him thanks for all the blessings He gives us. You can see, then, that the first purpose of our lives is the honor that we are to give to our God.

A second point is this: Since it is God's will to test our obedience as we live righteously among men, none of us should seek his own good but instead should seek to serve others. There should be mutual honesty among us, not only by abstaining from fraud, violence, and cruelty, but also by leading a sober and modest life, restrained, and without any obscenity or brutality. This is the second purpose of our lives.

Now we see why God specifically mentions that the Jews were in slavery in Egypt and why they are to have concern for those who are held captive by them. In those days servants were actually slaves and were treated like oxen and donkeys. For this reason, God tells the Jews that by keeping the Sabbath Day they will bring benefit and profit to their own family. Our Lord shows us the same thing that Jesus Christ taught in Matthew 6:33: If we seek the Kingdom of Heaven, all the other things will be given to us.

We seem to think that if we seek the heavenly life we will starve and be deprived of our other pleasures. But surely we cannot serve God unless we have cast off our own desires and have shaken off the worldly cares that press heavily on us. We must depend on the blessing that is promised to us, which is, that if we seek the Kingdom of God, we shall be blessed, even with these transient things. Nevertheless, men will not fail to find keeping it profitable to themselves. God will bless them for it, if they look to Him instead of eagerly seeking earthly pleasures.

We know what the pride of men is like; we all covet some form of recognition. Now if we are so arrogant that we find in our heart a desire to be elevated above our neighbors, even though there is no reason, what will we do if we are in fact elevated? We must observe that we are all made from one flesh (Genesis 9:6) and are all created in the image of God. If we realize that all those who are descended from Adam are our own flesh and bone, it ought to move us to kindness. But there is still more: The image of God is engraved in all men. Whenever I oppress any man, I not only despise myself but defile God's image as it remains in me. In this text God meant to show all those having authority and esteem, all who are richer than most, and any who have some degree of honor that they should not abuse those who are under their hand. When we come to our Lord Jesus Christ and look at Him, we must follow Him. Considering that all of us, both great and small, are members of His body and He is our Head, every one of us should adapt himself to his neighbors.

Let us now consider those who are not members of the Jewish nation but only conducting business among them. God also wants them to keep the Sabbath Day, even though they are not sanctified by God. If foreigners were permitted to carry out their business among the Jews, what would have been the result? The Jews would have traded with them and defiled themselves. When the occasion arises, we are easily led to do evil. Thus, if liberty had been given to foreigners to work and carry on business among the people of Israel on the Sabbath Day, it would have led to corruption. Therefore, to cut short the occasion for evil and to have the day observed with great reverence, God dealt with foreigners in the same way that He dealt with the beasts which He commanded to rest.

This commandment serves us also. It shows us that vices must not be permitted among people who profess to be Christians. They should not go unpunished, even among those who are foreigners and passing through. Let us note that our Lord intends to keep His people living in purity, so that those who profess to be Christians will not only abstain from evil themselves but will also not permit others to do evil, to the extent that this is possible.

It was not without purpose that our Lord required that the strangers who dwelt among His people were to be compelled to keep the seventh day. This was not for their own sakes or for their own instruction, but so that a stumbling block would not be placed in front of His own people. It was so that the land He had given as an inheritance to His servant Abraham might be entirely dedicated to Himself.

We are warned to keep ourselves holy in God's Word but also not to allow any occasion for an offense or corruption to be committed among us. Because our Lord wants us to be zealous in keeping pure our worship of Him, what excuse will we give if we do not give ourselves entirely to Him or behave in such a way that we are mirrors for drawing and winning poor unbelievers to our God?

Note:
Translated into modern English by James R. Hughes, from the *Sermons of John Calvin Upon the Fifth Book of Moses Called Deuteronomy*, translated from the French by Arthur Golding in 1583.

THE DANGER OF RICHES

John Wesley
(1703–1791)

They that will be rich fall into temptation and a snare,
and into many foolish and hurtful lusts,
which drown men in destruction and perdition.
1 TIMOTHY 6:9

How innumerable are the ill consequences that have followed from men's not knowing or not considering this great truth! How small is the number of those, even among real Christians, who understand and lay it to heart! Most pass it over, and many put such a construction upon it as to make it of no effect. "They that will be rich," say they, "that is, will be rich at all events, who will be rich right or wrong; that are resolved to carry their point, to compass this end, whatever means they use to attain it; they 'fall into temptation,' and into all the evils enumerated by the apostle."

The apostle does not speak here of gaining riches unjustly, but of quite another thing: His words are to be taken in their plain obvious sense, without any restriction or qualification whatsoever. St. Paul does not say, "They that will be rich by evil means, by theft, robbery, oppression, or extortion; they that will be rich by fraud or dishonest art"; but simply, "they that will be rich": These "fall into temptation and a snare, and into many foolish and hurtful lusts, which drown men in destruction and perdition."

But who believes that? Who preaches this strange doctrine? I have myself touched upon it in preaching, and twice in what I have published, but I have never published or preached expressly upon the subject. It is high time I should, in order to leave a full and clear testimony behind me whenever it pleases God to call me hence. O that God would give me to speak right and forcible words and you to receive them in honest and humble hearts!

First, let us consider what it is to be rich.

Whoever has sufficient food to eat and raiment to put on, with a place to lay his head and something left over, is rich. What is implied in the expression, "They that will be rich"? All those who endeavor after not only as much worldly substance as will procure them the necessaries and conveniences of life, but more than this.

Must we not, thirdly, rank among those that desire to be rich all that "lay up treasures on earth"? We are allowed to provide necessaries and conveniences for those of our own household. Men in business are to lay up as much as is necessary for the carrying on of that business. We are to leave our children what will supply them with necessaries and conveniences after we have left the world. We are to "owe no man anything." But to lay up any more the Lord has flatly forbidden.

We must rank among them, fourthly, all who

possess more of this world's goods than they use according to the will of the Donor. He only lends them to us as stewards, reserving the property of them to Himself. If we keep more of them in our hands than is necessary for the preceding purposes, we certainly fall under the charge of "desiring to be rich."

Under this imputation of "desiring to be rich," fall, fifthly, all "lovers of money." The word properly means those that delight in money; those that take pleasure in it. If there are any vices which are not natural to man, I should imagine this is one. Money of itself does not seem to gratify any natural desire or appetite of the human mind. Who is able to receive these hard sayings? Only those taught of God. And whom does God teach? "If any man be willing to do His will, he shall know of the doctrine whether it be of God." Those who are otherwise minded will be so far from receiving it that they will not be able to understand it.

"They fall into temptation." This seems to mean much more than simply, "they are tempted." They enter into the temptation: They fall plump down into it. Its waves compass them about and cover them. Of those who enter into temptation, very few escape it. The few that do are sorely scorched, though not utterly consumed. If they escape at all, it is with deep wounds that are not easily healed.

They fall, secondly, "into a snare"—the snare of the devil, which he hath set in their way. As soon as any creature touches the spring, it suddenly closes and either crushes its bones in pieces or consigns it to inevitable ruin.

They fall, thirdly, "into many foolish and hurtful desires." What desires are these? This is a most important question and deserves the deepest consideration. In general they may all be summed up in one—desiring happiness of God. St. Paul expresses it by "loving the creature more than the Creator" and by being "lovers of pleasure more than lovers of God." In particular they are "the desire of the flesh, the desire of the eyes, and the pride of life"; all of which the desire of riches tends to beget and increase. Riches lead to some of these foolish and hurtful desires and tend to increase them. There is a near connection between unholy desires and every other unholy passion and temper. We easily pass from these to pride, anger, bitterness, envy, malice, revengefulness; to a headstrong, unadvisable, unreprovable spirit: indeed to every temper that is earthly, sensual, or devilish. All these the desire or possession of riches naturally tends to create, strengthen, and increase.

I ask, in the name of God, who of you desire to be rich? Which of you seriously and deliberately desire to have more than food to eat and raiment to put on and a house to cover you? Who of you desires to have more than the plain necessaries and conveniences of life? Stop! What are you doing? By the grace of God, turn and live! By the same authority I ask, Who of you are endeavoring to be rich? to procure for yourselves more than the plain necessaries and conveniences of life? I ask, thirdly, who of you are in fact "laying up for yourselves treasures upon earth"? As long as you do well unto thyself, men will speak good of thee. Such is, and always has been, the wisdom of the world. But God says unto you, " 'Thou fool!' art thou not 'treasuring up to thyself wrath against the day of wrath, and revelation of the righteous judgment of God?' "

Perhaps you will ask, "But do not you yourself advise to gain all we can and to save all we can? Is it possible to do this without desiring and endeavoring to be rich?" I answer, It is possible.

You may gain all you can without hurting either your soul or body. You may save all you can by carefully avoiding every needless expense and yet never lay up treasures on earth or desire or endeavor so to do. I gain all I can (namely, by writing) without hurting either my soul or body. I save all I can, not willingly wasting anything—not a sheet of paper, not a cup of water. I do not lay out anything, not a shilling, unless as a sacrifice to God.

But some may say, "Whether you endeavor it or no, you are undeniably rich. You have more than the necessaries of life." I have, but I never desired or endeavored after it. And now that it is come upon me unawares, I lay up no treasures upon earth. I lay up nothing at all.

Having gained all you can and saved all you can, give all you can. Provide things needful for yourself; provide these for your wife, your children, your servants, or any others who pertain to your household. If, there is a surplus, then do good to "them that are of the household of faith." If there still be a surplus, "as you have opportunity, do good unto all men." You render unto God the things that are God's, not only by what you give to the poor, but also by that which you expend in providing things needful for yourself and your household.

Can you say,

I nothing want beneath, above;
Happy, happy in Thy love!

If your love of God is in anywise decayed, so is your love of your neighbor. You are then hurt in the very life and spirit of your religion! If you lose love, you lose all. You are so deeply hurt that you have well nigh lost your zeal for works of mercy, as well as of piety. You once pushed on through cold or rain to see the poor, the sick, the distressed. You went about doing good and found those who were not able to find you. You cheerfully crept down into their cellars and climbed up into their garrets,

To supply all their wants,
And spend and be spent in assisting His saints.

You found out every scene of human misery, and assisted according to your power:

Each form of woe your generous pity moved;
Your Savior's face you saw, and, seeing, loved.

Do you now tread in the same steps? What hinders? Are you not afraid of Him that hath said, "Inasmuch as ye have not done it unto the least of these, ye have not done it unto me"? Which of you now has that compassion for the ignorant and for them that are out of the way? They may wander on and plunge into the lake of fire without hindrance. Gold hath steeled your hearts. I have I given you, O ye gainers, lovers, possessors of riches, one more (it may be the last) warning. O that it may not be in vain! May God write it upon all your hearts!

SPIRITUAL WARNING

TEMPTATION

D. L. Moody
(1837–1899)

Watch ye and pray,
lest ye enter into temptation.
The spirit truly is ready,
but the flesh is weak.
MARK 14:38

One of the most real things in this world is temptation, and the quicker we find it out, the better.

When Christ was in the Garden of Gethsemane praying and His disciples were asleep, He woke them up and said to them: "Watch ye, and pray, lest ye enter into temptation. The spirit truly is ready, but the flesh is weak."

I don't suppose that one of those eleven men believed his flesh was weak. Jesus spoke these words to the three that were in the inner circle—Peter, James, and John. No doubt they thought, "There is no danger of our falling." But one of the twelve had already fallen, though they didn't know it yet. Peter, the chief speaker of the twelve, would that very night say that he never knew Him. John and James were to leave Him, for "all forsook Him and fled." You probably couldn't find eleven better men on the face of the earth than those eleven; and yet Christ warned them that the spirit was willing, but the flesh was weak. There has never been a man that has trod this earth that has not fallen sometime in his life, except the Man Christ Jesus.

Those eleven men were to be tempted that night as never before, and when the testing time came, every one of them fell. Oh, that God may open our eyes to see how very weak the flesh is!

A friend from Scotland said to me, speaking of a place where I had been, "Some time ago they had a storm that blew down between four and five thousand of the finest trees on that old estate. Do you know why? Because the storm came in an unexpected direction. It had never come from that quarter before. It had blown in every direction but that one, and the forest wasn't prepared, and away the trees went."

It is said that Edinburgh Castle was never taken but once. Then the enemy came up the steep rocks at a place the garrison thought was so safe they needn't guard it. Very often temptation comes in an unexpected form or from an unexpected quarter, when you are off your guard; hence the necessity of watching and praying, because if you are not on the alert, you will be tripped up by the tempter.

Scripture adds: "Let him that thinketh he standeth, take heed lest he fall." No man on earth is beyond the reach of the tempter. The tempter will follow you from the cradle to the grave, and the nearer you get to Christ, the hotter the fight will be. The temptations that come to you and me are common to man. Every man before us has had the same kind of temptation, although it may come to us in a different way. There are four great temptations that threaten us today.

First, the theater.

A prominent and wealthy elder of a church in the West, who used to say that I was bigoted and narrow-minded and puritanical in my ideas about the stage, had a son who got married. Soon afterwards a woman came along, put a bullet through his heart, and killed him. He had got acquainted with her at the theater, and she claimed him.

I would rather be narrow and right than broad and wrong. I don't want to take my two sons into a place where they will be tempted. I wouldn't give a snap of my finger for a Christian that goes to all these places of amusement and offsets his testimony. It is one thing to pray God to fill you with the Spirit, but if He does, you must be separated from the world. You don't want your daughter or sister on the stage, do you? You wouldn't like to see your mother there. Then why patronize someone else's sister? Why encourage someone else's wife?

But you say, "I know a number of good people that go."

So do I, but I know a number of people that have to reap in their children. It is easy enough for the father and mother to take their children in the way of temptation, but when they want to get them away, it is a different thing.

You must be separated from the world if you want power.

But you say, "I shall lose influence." Do you know the difference between influence and power? I will tell you. Ahab had influence; Elijah had power. Strive for influence with the world, if you want to, but it will die when you die. Where is Ahab's influence today? Where is Nebuchadnezzar's influence, and the whole crowd of them, compared with Elijah's and Daniel's? Daniel has been gone these twenty-five hundred years, and still he shines, and is going to shine forever. He overcame temptation.

Another great temptation is to disregard the Sabbath.

We have a good deal worse foe than any foreign power right in our midst. This country will go to pieces if we give up the Sabbath. No country has existed a great while and been prosperous that has wiped out the Sabbath. It is easy to destroy, to tear down, but it is a thousand times better to build up.

One great means of Sabbath-breaking is the bicycle.

"Oh," you say, "what is the matter with the bicycle? Isn't it a great blessing?"

Yes; and like all good blessings it can be turned into a curse by misuse. I was in Brooklyn not long ago, and I saw something that was a revelation to me. Right opposite the church where I was to preach, a bicycle club started off for a run at half past ten, just as people were going to church. A few years ago that wouldn't have been countenanced in Brooklyn, the city of churches. It wasn't the scum of Brooklyn that were there, but some of the leading young men. And in that church where I preached there hardly seemed to be twenty-five young men.

Your bicycle can be a blessing, but when you go off and spend God's day in recreation and neglect the house of God, what will become of your soul? Are you not putting yourself in the way of temptation? "Remember the Sabbath day to keep it holy." Do not turn God's holy day into a holiday.

Then there are the Sunday newspapers. I would not dare to ask how many of you read the Sunday newspapers. You think you must have them to find out the news. They have sermons, too; fine sermons. Someone took pains to look over seven of the New York Sunday papers awhile ago, and this is what he found in them: Nine hundred and eleven and a quarter total columns, and only three and a quarter columns of them religious. That is Sunday reading! Gabriel himself couldn't hold an audience whose heads were full of such stuff as that.

There was a time when a man used to lock up his store Saturday night and have a rest on the Sabbath, but now he locks up his store, puts a flaming advertisement in the Sunday paper, and does a bigger business than any other day in the week. Men, where is your conscience? I hope it will smite you the next time you offer to patronize a Sunday paper.

A man will walk right into temptation and then wonder why he isn't kept from it. What the world needs is men who will face these issues and stand by the right, even if he has to stand alone.

Then there is a fourth temptation: false doctrines and false teachers.

I asked an atheist some years ago how he accounted for the creation of the world.

"Well," he said, "force and matter worked together and by chance the world came out."

That is as clear as mud to me. It is strange a man's toes are not sticking on the top of his head if things were thrown together in that way.

A man won't believe that a watch was made without a maker, but we have more absurd doctrines. Some people would have us believe that there is no matter anyway. A man thinks he exists, but he doesn't! What is to me still more awful is that they say there is no such thing as sin. I asked a lady who held this doctrine what she would call it if I should willfully and in cold blood take the life of a friend.

"It would be an error of judgment," was her answer.

Between 1895–98 we had in this country 38,512 murders, while England in the same length of time had less than 600. Think of it! Less than 300 lives were lost on the *Maine,* and every twenty-four hours 300 in this country reel into drunkards' graves. And yet there are men and women teaching that there is no such thing as sin! O come forward and stand against these false doctrines like men.

The temptations are all around us, but blessed is he that endureth temptation—not, "Blessed is he that is tried and tempted," but "he that endureth, for when he is tried he shall receive a crown of life."

DEATH AND ETERNITY

The Second Coming

Billy Sunday
(1862–1935)

Then we which are alive and remain shall be
caught up together with them in the clouds,
to meet the Lord in the air:
and so shall we ever be with the Lord.
Wherefore comfort one another with these words.
1 Thessalonians 4:17–18

No meeting ever held anywhere or at any time can begin to compare with the greatest of all meetings to be held in the air when our Lord comes to make up His jewels. All that has been done in this world up to the present time has been in preparation for that great meeting.

We are not told when Jesus will come, but we are told that His coming is sure, and we are charged to watch for it.

A great many say, "I believe the millennium will come first, then Christ will come at the end of it." What people think has nothing to do with it; what God says has everything to do with it. You will see God's time card if you carefully read the Bible. It gives only the slightest hope for the millennium before the return of Christ; but you can find plenty of verses that tell you to look for the coming of the Lord first. There can be no millennium until Jesus comes; it is His presence that makes the millennium. The glory of God shall cover the earth, but it will be after Jesus comes.

When Jesus first came, the smallest predictions were fulfilled to the very letter. Should this not teach us to expect that the same will be true when He comes again? John Bunyan was once studying the passages foretelling that the feet of the Lord should stand on the Mount of Olives, and he thus reasoned: "Some commentators say that the Mount of Olives means the heart of the believer; that it is only a figurative expression and means that the Lord will reign in the heart of the believer, and the Holy Spirit will dwell there. But I don't think it means that at all. I just think it means the Mount of Olives, two miles from Jerusalem, on the east." And that is why the Lord could use the poor tinker so marvelously, even when he was shut up in Bedford jail.

Jesus taught His disciples to be in constant expectation of His early return, and they lived accordingly. They preached the doctrine and taught it in their epistles. Certainly, if anybody ever understood the Lord correctly, it was the men whom He personally trained, that they might hand down the truth He gave them.

Jesus is going to come and reveal Himself to the members of His body at the very moment when the last soul is saved necessary to complete that body—for the body of Christ must consist of a certain number of souls, or it never could be completed. He can no more come without His heavenly body than He could come the first time without a human body. The completion of the body of Christ will bring Him. Every time we do personal work or try to get anybody saved, we may be doing something that will bring the coming of the Lord. Instead of being discouraged by seeing what a small prospect there is of the whole world being converted, it will set our bones on fire to think that perhaps the last man needed to complete the Lord's body and bring Jesus back to earth may be converted this very day.

God's purpose for this dispensation is the completing of the body of Christ. That is the present dispensation, and that is what God is doing now. The mission of the church is to get ready to meet the Bridegroom. When the body of Christ is completed, He will reveal Himself to the members who are alive and in this world at that time, and at the same moment they will be caught up to meet those who have gone on before in the air, and from that moment they are forever with the Lord. The body of Christ will be composed of believers from every race and nation on earth. That is why the gospel must first be preached as a witness to every nation. It had its beginning on the day of Pentecost and will be complete at the time of the meeting in the air, which is called the Rapture, for He is now preparing, perfecting, and completing the Church—the body of Christ, the bride who is to meet the Lord in the air and be with Him forevermore.

The moment the last one is saved, Christ will be

revealed—not to the world, but to His Church—His bride. When the Rapture comes, it will be altogether unexpected, except by those who have been searching the prophecies and are looking for it. The remainder of the world will not know that He has been here, and they will not know what has become of the missing ones. But things will soon settle back into their old condition, and the world will go on its way.

The notion people have about the second coming of Christ is that when He comes, the Judgment Day will also come, and the world will come to an end. This idea is unscriptural. Business will go on, and governments will go on as now. After Jesus comes and takes the believers out of the world, then comes the Great Tribulation. At the close of the Tribulation, the Lord will return, bringing with Him His saintly members of His body, to begin His millennium reign. Then He will reveal Himself to the Jews. They will accept Him as their long-rejected Messiah. Then the millennium will begin; the devil will be cast into the bottomless pit for a thousand years, and nations will be born in a day through the missionary efforts of the Jews.

Either before or during the Tribulation, the Jews will be restored to the Holy Land, rebuilding their temple and restoring Jewish worship. Also during the Tribulation the Antichrist will come, most likely in the person of some great king. He will go to Jerusalem and do great signs and wonders by which he will so delude the chosen people that they will accept him as their Messiah and pay him divine honors in the temple. It will be during this that Jesus will return and destroy him by the brightness of His coming.

If we are so fortunate as to have a part in that meeting in the air, it will mean that we have lived in the most blessed of all times, for only those who live in the present dispensation are eligible to membership in the body of Christ. Some who are born into this world are never to die, and we may hope to be of that elect number. It will also mean that we shall then have bodies that will remain young forever. Pains and aches, gray hair, wrinkles, and feebleness will never again be known. Others, from the most grinding poverty, will spring to eternal wealth. As we look about us now, it looks as if that great time will never come. But you can't tell by appearances. All signs point to the great event, some of which seem to me to be:

(a) Radical tendency to depart from the Christian faith.
(b) Prophecies fulfilled—the gospel has been preached in every nation.
(c) The worldwide expectancy of His coming.
(d) Revival among the Jews. They are flocking to Jerusalem.
(e) Political unrest.
(f) Extreme views on questions of government.
(g) Concentration of wealth in the hands of the few.

If we have a part in that meeting, we shall be in

this world with the Lord during the millennium, with the devil chained and cast out. To have part in that meeting will be to meet those who have gone on before—fathers and mothers and other loved ones. There will be no devil to cause human suffering and woe. If we have a part in that meeting, we shall escape the Great Tribulation which is to come upon all the earth. The body of Christ is now the army with which God holds in check the principalities and powers of evil. When this army is taken out of the world, the devil will have unhindered sway. Do you want to live in that kind of time? Well, the only thing that can save you from it is to have a part in that meeting in the air. It is supposed that the Tribulation will cover a period of seven years. It might be seven hundred years; but it cannot be less than seven years. God in His mercy will make it as short as possible.

When will the meeting in the air occur? Jesus said, "But of that day and that hour knoweth no man, no, not the angels which are in heaven, neither the Son, but the Father. Take ye heed, watch and pray: for ye know not when the time is" (Mark 13:32–33). At the close of the millennium reign of Christ, the devil will be loosed out of the pit for a season and look upon a world without sin. He will tempt people. They will be as foolish as now and yield to his lies and subtlety. He will gather his host and come against the saints to battle. Fire will fall from heaven and consume them. Then takes place the resurrection of the wicked dead, followed by the judgment of the great white throne, with Christ to judge. We are not told when Jesus will come, but we are told that His coming is sure, and we are charged to watch for it.

"COME, LORD JESUS!"

MANY MANSIONS

Jonathan Edwards
(1703–1758)

In my Father's house are many mansions.
JOHN 14:2

Christ spoke to His disciples in the foregoing chapter as
one that was about to leave them. He told them, in
verse 31, "Now is the Son of man glorified, and God is
glorified in him," and then gave them counsel to live in
unity and love one another, as one that was going from
them. They seemed somewhat surprised and hardly
knew what to make of this. Peter asked Him where He
was going, and Christ did not directly answer, but in
verse 12 He tells them plainly that He was going to His
Father.

We may observe the description of God's house:
In it there are many mansions. The disciples seemed
very sorrowful at the news of Christ's going away, but
Christ comforts them by saying that in His Father's
house there was not only room for Him, but room for
them too. There were many mansions. When the disciples perceived that Christ was going away, they
manifested a great desire to go with Him, particularly
Peter. In the latter part of the foregoing chapter, Peter
asked Jesus where He was going, so he might follow
Him. Christ told him that he could not follow Him

now, but that he should follow Him afterwards. Peter seemed determined to follow Him now. "Lord," says he, "why cannot I follow thee now?" Christ intimates that they shall be with Him in due time, in that there were many mansions there. There was a mansion provided not only for Him, but for them all (Judas was not then present), and not only for them, but for all that should ever believe in Him to the end of the world. Though He went before, He only went to prepare a place for them that should follow.

There are two propositions contained in these words: that heaven is God's house, and that in this house of God there are many mansions.

A house of public worship is where God's people meet from time to time to attend on God's ordinances. It is set apart for that and called God's house. The temple of Solomon was called God's house; God was represented as dwelling there. There He has His throne in the holy of holies, even the mercy seat over the ark and between the cherubims.

But the highest heaven is especially represented in Scripture as the house of God. We are told that the heavens are the Lord's, but the earth He hath given to the sons of men. Houses where assemblies of Christians worship God are in some respects figures of this house of God above. When God is worshipped in them in spirit and truth, they become the outworks of heaven. As in houses of public worship, there are assemblies of Christians meeting to worship God, so in heaven there is a glorious assembly, or Church, continually worshipping God (Hebrews 12:22–23).

Heaven is the house where God dwells with His family. God has many children, and the place designed for them is heaven; therefore the saints, being the children of God, are said to be of the household of God, Ephesians 2:19: "Now therefore ye are no more strangers and foreigners, but fellowcitizens with the saints, and of the household of God." Heaven is the house not only where God has His throne, but also where He keeps His table, where His children sit down with Him at His table, and where they are feasted in a royal manner becoming the children of so great a King.

There are many mansions in the house of God— many seats or places of abode. Kings' houses are wont to be built very large, with many stately rooms. When this is spoken of heaven, it is chiefly to be understood in a figurative sense, and the following things seem to be taught us in it.

There is room in this house of God for great numbers. There is in heaven a sufficiency for the happiness of every sort; there is a convenient accommodation for every creature that will hearken to the calls of the gospel. None that will come to Christ need to fear but that Christ will provide a place suitable for him in heaven.

This seems to be another thing implied in Christ's words. The disciples were of very different condition from Christ, but though they were in such different circumstances from Him, yet Christ encourages them that there shall not only be room in heaven for Him, but for them too; for there were many mansions there.

When God made heaven in the beginning of the world, He intended it for an everlasting dwellingplace for a vast and innumerable multitude. When it is said, "In my Father's house are many mansions," it is meant that there are seats of various dignity and different degrees and circumstances of honor and happiness. Some are designed to sit in higher places than others; some are designed to be advanced to higher degrees of honor and glory. Therefore there are various mansions in heaven, and some more honorable mansions and seats. Not that we are to understand the words of Christ in a literal sense, as that every saint in heaven was to have a certain seat or room or place of abode where he was to be locally fixed. We are to understand what Christ says chiefly in a spiritual sense. Persons shall be set in different degrees of honor and glory in heaven. Some seats shall be nearer the throne than others. Some shall sit next to Christ in glory.

But I would improve this doctrine in a twofold exhortation.

Let all be hence exhorted earnestly to seek that they may be admitted to a mansion in heaven. You have heard that this is God's house; it is His temple. If David so longed that he might return to the land of Israel that he might have a place in the house of God here on earth, how great a happiness will it be to have a place in this heavenly temple of God!

You now have a house or mansion of your own, or at least one that is for your use, but how little a while will this continue! Your stay is as it were but for a night. Your body itself is but a house of clay which will quickly moulder and tumble down, and you shall have no other habitation here in this world but the grave. Consider: When you die, if you have no mansion in the house of God in heaven, you must have your place of abode in the habitation of devils. There is no middle place between them, and when you go hence, you must go to one or the other of these.

If you die unconverted, you will have the worse place in hell for having had a seat or place in God's house in this world. As there are many mansions, places of different degrees of honor in heaven, so there are various abodes and places or degrees of torment and misery in hell; and those will have the worst place there that, dying unconverted, have had the best place in God's house here.

The second exhortation that I would offer is to seek a high place in heaven. Seeing there are many mansions of different degrees of honor and dignity in heaven, seek to obtain a mansion of distinguished glory. It is not becoming of persons to be overanxious about a high seat in God's house in this world, for that is the honor that is of men; but we can't too earnestly seek after a high seat in God's house above by seeking eminent holiness, for that is the honor that is of God. The mansions in God's house above are everlasting mansions. Those that have seats allotted them there will hold them to all eternity. This is promised, Revelation 3:12: "Him that overcometh will I make a pillar in the temple of my God, and he shall go no more out."

Let the main thing that we prize in God's house be not the outward ornaments of it or a high seat in it, but the Word of God and His ordinances in it. And spend your time here in seeking Christ, that He may prepare a place for you in His Father's house, that when He comes again to this world, He may take you to Himself, that where He is, there you may be also.

Inspirational Library

Beautiful purse/pocket-size editions of Christian classics bound in flexible leatherette. These books make thoughtful gifts for everyone on your list, including yourself!

When I'm on My Knees The highly popular collection of devotional thoughts on prayer, especially for women.
  Flexible Leatherette $4.97

The Bible Promise Book Over 1,000 promises from God's Word arranged by topic. What does God promise about matters like: Anger, Illness, Jealousy, Love, Money, Old Age, and Mercy? Find out in this book!
  Flexible Leatherette $3.97

Daily Wisdom for Women A daily devotional for women seeking biblical wisdom to apply to their lives. Scripture taken from the New American Standard Version of the Bible.
  Flexible Leatherette $4.97

My Daily Prayer Journal Each page is dated and features a Scripture verse and ample room for you to record your thoughts, prayers, and praises. One page for each day of the year.
  Flexible Leatherette $4.97

Available wherever books are sold.
Or order from:

Barbour Publishing, Inc.
P.O. Box 719
Uhrichsville, OH 44683
www.barbourbooks.com

If you order by mail, add $2.00 to your order for shipping.
Prices are subject to change without notice.